ARE THERE BIBLE CONTRADICTIONS: AN APOLOGETIC RESPONSE

PERSEUS POKU

Are There Bible Contradictions: An Apologetic Response

Copyright © 2024 by Perseus Poku. No portion of this work may be reproduced, stored in a retrieval system, or transmitted in any form or by any means–electronic, mechanical, photocopy, recording, or other- except for a brief quotation in printed review, without the prior permission of the publisher. All rights reserved.

ISBN: 979-8-218-45490-6

DEDICATION

This book is dedicated to my wife, Keyna. Your unwavering support and prayers have been the cornerstone of my journey, enabling me to focus on the divine assignment that God has entrusted me with. I am forever grateful for your love and encouragement.

TABLE OF CONTENTS

I. 2 Reasons Why Bible verses Seem Like Contradictions ...3
II. What is a Paradox?..5
III. 10 Examples of Apparent Contradictions in the Bible.......7
IV. Working Through Examples of Apparent
    Contradictions 11
V. Conclusion..15
VI. Hermeneutics..17

PREFACE

The Bible is one of the most purchased books in the world. Christians argue that God is the author of the Bible. We also believe that God is perfect. As a result, His word (the Bible) must be free from error (inerrant). However, some skeptics claim that the Bible is filled with contradictions (errors). If this is true, then what we believe about the Bible cannot be trusted. This book was written to help believers understand the reality of paradoxes and how to read the Bible from a hermeneutical lens.

ARE THERE CONTRADICTIONS IN THE BIBLE? AN APOLOGIST'S ANSWER

The Bible tells us that all Scripture is authored by God (2 Tim 3:16). This implies that the Scriptures are also without error since God is the author and he is without error. However, we often encounter Bible passages that seem to contradict each other.

These passages are hard to understand. Because of that difficulty, some can be quick to believe that what they're reading is a contradiction. Others may expect or already believe these verses don't contradict each other—yet they can't explain how to reconcile them. (Continue reading for assistance in that area.)

2 REASONS WHY BIBLE VERSES SEEM LIKE CONTRADICTIONS

I would argue that the appearance of contradictory verses results from the reader's interpretation.

Christian author and theologian.

William Arndt wrote the following regarding this subject:

The difficulties which are pointed to in the Bible by its friends and its foes are of many kinds. The great majority of them are entirely of the person's own making and will vanish when prayerfully studied. 1

The apostle Peter also suggests that there are some passages we do not understand due to our ignorance (2 Pet 3:16).

And count the patience of our Lord as salvation, just as our beloved brother Paul also wrote to you according to the wisdom given him, as he does in all his letters when he speaks in them of these matters. Some things in them are hard to understand, which the ignorant and unstable twist to their destruction, as they do the other Scriptures. (2 Pet 3:15–16)

In other words, we may need to learn more about a passage before we can understand it.

Another source of seeming contradictions is ourselves—who we are, our hearts and minds. As evangelist and Pastor R. A. Torrey argues,

The Bible is perfect, but we, being imperfect, have difficulty with it. As we grow more and more into the perfection of God, our difficulties grow ever less and less, and so we are forced to conclude that when we become as perfect as God is, we shall have no more difficulties whatever with the Bible. 2

My goal here is to make clear that the Bible does not contain contradictions but **paradoxes.**

WHAT IS A PARADOX?

A paradox is a perceived contradiction that, upon further study, is found to be harmonious.

Conflicts arise when it seems the Bible says two different things about the same subject. However, when we employ simple Bible interpretation techniques, we soon realize that the verses are in harmony.

Both testaments contain perceived contradictions—paradoxes. These areas of perceived contradictions cover topics such as culture, language, morality, eschatology, worship, and many other doctrinal issues.

10 EXAMPLES OF APPARENT CONTRADICTIONS IN THE BIBLE

Statement	Bible verse	"Contradictory" statement	Bible verse
God is jealous	Exodus 20:5	God is void of jealousy	Proverbs 6:34
God tempts men	Genesis 22:1	God does not tempt men	James 1:13
God is unchangeable	Numbers 23:19	God changes his plans	1 Samuel 15:10–11
Jesus is equal to the Father	Philippians 2:5–6	Jesus says "The Father is greater than I"	John 14:26
God judges	John 5:22, 27	God does not judge	John 12:47
There is no one that is sinless	Romans 3:10	Job was perfect and upright	Job 1:1
We are justified by faith	Romans 3:20	We are justified by works	James 2:14
The dead will be raised	Isaiah 26:19	The dead will not rise	Job 14:12
Once a person dies there is no return from the grave	Luke 16:19–31	Samuel returned from the grave	1 Samuel 28:11–20
The Christian will not sin	1 John 5:18	The Christian will sin	1 John 1:10

How to consider these passages: An Introduction to Bible Interpretation

To overcome perceived contradictions in the Bible, turn to observation and interpretation.

Observation allows you to inspect the passage without judgment.

You are looking simply for information. Observe the content and context of the passage.

1. Ask these questions:
   a. Who are the main characters in the passage?
   b. What is going on?
   c. When and where did the events occur?
2. Look up the meaning of the words in the verses.
3. Look at the literary context and the placement of words.

The same word can mean something different based on its surrounding words. For example, the word "trunk" in English can have multiple meanings based on its context. If we say, "I placed my winter clothes in the trunk," we know it is a trunk used for storage.

In contrast, if we say, "Do not water around the base of the trunk," we know we are talking about the trunk of a tree and not a storage unit. In the same way, word usage in the Bible is based on context.

1. Consider the culture, language, history, and religious beliefs.

    Use the information gleaned from the observation phase to interpret the passage.

Do further word study by asking these questions: "What is the meaning of the word in its original language?" and "How was it used in ancient times?"

Finally, ask, "What is the overall principle that can be adopted by contemporary Christians?"

This is not a process exclusive to scholars or theologians—every Christian can rightly divide the Word of God.

★★★

Tools to help with Bible interpretation

If you're wondering how to learn more about culture, context, history, etc., these three types of resources are excellent places to start: study Bibles, Bible dictionaries, and Bible commentaries.

An excellent way to combine all of these <u>Bible study tools</u> in one and get powerful features to help you use them is to get a <u>Bible app</u> like Logos. It's free and available for <u>web</u>, <u>mobile</u>, and <u>desktop</u>.

Bible Tips:

In order to avoid confusion about a text, one must use Bible tools. Consider the following passage found in the gospel of Luke.

"If anyone comes to Me and does not hate his own father, mother, wife, children, brothers, sisters, yes, and even his own life, he cannot be My disciple."-Luke 14:26 (King James Version).

If we read it in English, it seems contradictory. We know God is love, and He desires us to obey our parents (Ephesians

6:13). It seems the passage in Luke tells us to hate our parents, while Ephesians tells us to honor our parents. How do we resolve this dilemma? The short answer is context, context, context.

Your first step is to define the Greek word used by the King James Version of the Bible. Grab a Bible dictionary or a Strong's Exhaustive Concordance of the Bible. When we look at the Strong's Concordance, we learn that the Greek word for "hate" is "miseo." Based on the Greek lexicon, we learn that the word "miseo" means to "love less." If we take this meaning and apply it to Luke 14:26, we learn that Jesus is not saying to hate or despise our parents. It is saying if you want to follow Jesus, you have to love less your mother and father. In short, Jesus has to be first.

★★★

WORKING THROUGH EXAMPLES OF APPARENT CONTRADICTIONS

There are numerous Bible paradoxes, but we will work through the following well-known apparent contradictions together.

Proverbs 26:4 and Proverbs 26:5

When compared, Proverbs 26:4 and 26:5 seem to contradict the author (Solomon). Verse 4 says not to answer a fool, but verse 5 seems to suggest that a fool should be answered.

But this is a paradox, not a contradiction. Here's why: Proverbs 26:4 speaks against engaging someone who is foolish. Arguing with a fool or irrational person will draw you into their web, and you will become foolish yourself.

Verse 5 speaks of engaging a fool in another sense. There are times when a foolish person must be corrected, or things will continue to get worse. In this case, we are providing godly wisdom to the fool and not quarreling with them, as in verse 4. It would only be contradictory if verse 4 stated that we should never speak to a fool at any time.

Matthew 5:6 and John 6:35

We can also find what might seem a contradiction when we compare Matthew 5:6 and John 6:35. Matthew 5:6 tells us that those who do hunger for righteousness are blessed.

However, John 6:35 seems to say the opposite. John 6:35 quotes Jesus as saying, "The one who comes to me will not be hungry." Matthew writes that a follower of Christ will be blessed if they hunger. However, John's Gospel suggests that if we believe in Jesus, we will never be hungry.

Bible observation and interpretation again show that these verses are in harmony. In Matthew 5:6, Jesus uses physical examples to illustrate spiritual principles. In the same way that hunger compels us to seek food and thirstiness to seek water, we need to seek righteousness. He is using physical realities to convey a spiritual concept.

In John 6:35, Jesus refers to himself as the "Bread of Life." This phrase is not to be taken literally. Jesus is not an actual loaf of bread. However, he uses this metaphor to convey a message. In the same way that bread satisfies the body, if his disciples follow him, they will receive spiritual food. Within this context, we find the next portion of the text. Because Jesus is the bread of life, those who follow and obey his teachings will not be hungry or thirsty as it relates to spiritual matters. Again, these two verses are not contradictory but complementary.

Romans 3:28 and James 2:24

Romans 3:28 tells us that a person is justified by faith alone and not by working for it. This passage seems clear.

However, when we read James' letter, we discover that James suggests that believers are justified by their works and not by faith alone.

Here's why this is not a contradiction. Paul is saying one is saved by faith and cannot work for it. On the other hand, James is appealing to those who are already saved. James argues that because they are already Christians, there must be an extension of their faith, as evidenced by what they do (works). Regarding this passage, Biblical scholar and linguist John Haley concluded:

There is no collision between Paul and James. They merely present different aspects or relations of the same great truth. Paul is arguing against self-righteous religionists, who rely for salvation upon external morality, upon mere works; James addresses those who maintain that, provided a man's belief is correct, it matters little what his conduct is; that a bare assertive faith is sufficient for salvation, without its living fruits in a holy life.[3]

CONCLUSION

The Bible contains passages that readers may find difficult to understand. Those passages may even seem contradictory. However, we must keep in mind that the Bible is inerrant (void of error).

If we see contradictions, it is due to our lack of understanding, and we must struggle with the text until arriving at the correct interpretation. Using the rules of observation and interpretation will help us to resolve any perceived contradictions we may encounter when reading the Scriptures.

★★★

1. William Arndt, *Bible Difficulties and Seeming Contradictions* (St. Louis, MO: Concordia Publishing House, 1987), 9–10.
2. R. A. Torrey, *Difficulties and Alleged Errors and Contradictions in the Bible* (Las Vegas, NV: Crossreach Publications, 2023), 19.
3. John Haley, *Alleged Errors of the Bible: Addressing Problematic Passages in Scripture* (New Kensington: Whitaker House Publishers, 2019), 147.

Conclusion: Hermeneutics

In order to respond Biblically to attacks against inerrancy, we must first know how to correctly read God's words. This requires learning more about hermeneutics (the science and art of Biblical interpretation). Following the rules that govern proper exegesis will lead you to sound doctrine. The following information will help you learn how to read and study the Scriptures better.

Unlocking the Bible: Effective Bible Study

Learn the structure of the Bible, the correct method for interpreting Scripture through proper exegesis, the resources for personal study, and other subjects that will add meaning to the reading of the Bible.

HERMENEUTICS

I. HERMENEUTICS

Hermeneutics is defined as the science and art of Biblical interpretation. In other words, there is a correct way of interpreting the Bible. Every believer's goal should be to have a desire to understand what the Scriptures are saying or not saying.

Many Christians are often misguided in their approach to understanding scriptural passages. The first question should not be, "What does the Bible mean to me?" The first question should be "What was the intended meaning to the original recipients of the letter?" Once we understand the original meaning to the intended recipients, we can discern if the message is descriptive or prescriptive. The difference between descriptive and prescriptive are as follows:

Hermeneutics: The Difference Between Descriptive and Prescriptive Texts

Descriptive texts are those passages that describe a one-time event. This means the act or commandment given in the story was not intended to be duplicated. These types of texts are told to describe an event that happened once. In addition, some commandments fall under the Descriptive category.

Let us take a look at some Descriptive passages:

"Now God worked unusual miracles by the hands of Paul, so that even handkerchiefs or aprons were brought from his body to the sick, and the diseases left them and the evil spirits went out of them."-Acts 19:11-12

One can look at this passage and erroneously assume that this passage is suggesting all Christians are able to heal others with a handkerchief. We know this is not the case because of the following:

1. We must first know the general theme of the book. In other words, what is the overall message of the composition? In relation to the book of Acts, the theme is "Jesus: the Risen Glorified Lord over All His Church." The miracles performed by the apostles were extraordinary and initiated by God for the 1st Century Christians. We must remember that God does not perform miracles for entertainment. God sometimes performs miracles through humans for two reasons: (A) to confirm His messenger (B) to confirm His message.

   God is not performing miracles arbitrarily. Miracles are done only for the two reasons above. In Acts 19, this is the reason for this supernatural act. Man does not initiate miracles; it is the prerogative of God. Paul could only heal with the handkerchief because that is what God wanted to do through him (Paul) for the sake of those around him. God knew that particular miracle would get the attention of those who were eyewitnesses. Luke, the writer of Acts wanted to capture the consistency of God. The same God that performed miracles through Jesus was doing the same thing through the apostles. This is what Christ was talking about when he said, "Verily, verily, I say unto you, He that believeth on me, the works that I do shall he also do; and greater works than these shall he do; because I go unto my Father."- John 14:12-14. Jesus was basically saying that you will see greater things not in importance but in quantity. In other words, God is going to do more supernatural things because there will be more disciples. This prophecy was fulfilled in the 1st Century, as evidenced by the stories depicted in the Book of Acts. Many of the miracles reported in Acts were for a one-time purpose based on the specific situation. In addition, the Scriptures do not tell us that God promises to administer the same miracles through All Christians.

2. If Acts 19 is to be interpreted for qualified saints having the ability to heal with handkerchiefs, then it would be prescriptive. Prescriptive means that it happens all the time for those believers who meet certain criteria (e.g., having genuine faith and being closer to God than others). However, this is not the case. The apostle Paul, who was chosen by God and healed others with a handkerchief, did not heal his friend Trophimus.

In 2 Timothy 4:20, Paul states he left Trophimus sick. This is the same Paul who has the gift of healing. This text proves that healing is not up to Paul but God. God decides who or when to heal. Healing is rooted in God's prerogative. We do not find any verse in the Bible that states God will heal all physical ailments. Moreover, we do not find any Scriptures that it is God's will to duplicate this unique one-time event of healing people with handkerchiefs.

How do we know if a text is Descriptive and not Prescriptive? Descriptive text, as I mentioned earlier, is a record of a one-time event or an event that was culturally based. This means the text is providing information for our historic edification, not for Christians to still follow or duplicate. Another good example of a Descriptive text is 1 Corinthians 11:1-6:

Paul writes: "Follow my example, as I follow the example of Christ. I praise you for remembering me in everything and holding to the traditions just as I passed them on to you. But I want you to realize that the head of every man is Christ, and the head of the woman is man, and the head of Christ is God. Every man who prays or prophesies with his head covered dishonors his head. But every woman who prays or prophesies with her head uncovered dishonors her head—it is the same as having her head shaved. For if a woman does not cover her head, she might as well have her hair cut off; but if it is a disgrace for a woman to have her hair cut off or her head shaved, then she should cover her head."

Is Paul saying all Christian women should cover their heads during worship? The answer is no! How do we know Paul is not making this prescriptive? The first clue is we do not find any other passage in the New Testament outside of the Corinthian church where Paul mandates these rules. This means we have to look at this passage (1 Corinthians 11) contextually. Context is everything. What was going on in the church of Corinth? What does having the head covered symbolize during those times? What message is Paul trying to convey as it relates to headship?

In order to remain faithful to my argument, I will not address the "headship" argument in regard to its etymology. My focus is specifically on the covering of the head. Paul emphatically forbade the man to have his head covered while worshipping. What does this mean? Is Paul saying it is sinful for a Christian man to wear a hat while worshipping? Again, we must look at the context and cultural paradigm of the 1st Century Corinthian church. Some argue that Paul denounced wearing a head covering for men of Corinth because head coverings were used by other men in Roman culture for pagan worship. In addition, it is probably not the case that Paul forbids Christian men to wear head garbs during worship.

Again, it is always important to look at a verse contextually. In addition, we must compare that text to the entire Bible. We find in the Old Testament that God actually instructed Aaron to wear a head garb (Exodus 29:6). So how should we reconcile these two verses? The short answer is that both verses are descriptive in nature and not intended for readers to try and follow the orders. How do we know this? We know this is the case due to what is going on in the story. In addition, there have to be additional passages that substantiate our conclusion. In this case, as we consider the cultural context the proper conclusion as it relates to men wearing head garbs during worship is descriptive rather than prescriptive. Conversely, Paul writes that women should have their heads covered. Paul connects not wearing a head covering to having their heads shaved. It has been reported that head shaving of women in the Mediterranean world was normally associated with the punishment of adulterous women. As a result, many believe Paul is saying Christian women should wear their veils in order to bring honor to their husbands and not dishonor.

Prescriptive Passages:

As I stated before, Prescriptive passages are those instructional passages that contain principles intended for ALL Christians. The method of identifying Prescriptive passages is the same as that for Descriptive passages. What is the context? Is there a cultural norm involved? Can we find evidence of the same principle in other passages? If you cannot find a corroborating passage, then the text may more than likely be Descriptive.

Examples of Prescriptive Passages:
> "This is what the LORD says—
> Israel's King and Redeemer, the LORD Almighty:
> I am the first and I am the last;
> apart from me there is no God.-Isaiah 44:6

We learn from Isaiah that there is only ONE God, this is a Prescriptive teaching. God intends for all believers to accept this reality. How do we know this is the case? We find the same principle again in Revelation.

"I am the Alpha and the Omega," says the Lord God, "who is, and who was, and who is to come, the Almighty."-Revelation 1:8.

Another Prescriptive passage is the teaching that men should always pray. We find it in at least two passages (Luke 18:1 & 1 Thessalonians 5:17).

The principle of obeying parents is found in both the Old and New Testaments.

"'Anyone who curses their father or mother is to be put to death. Because they have cursed their father or mother, their blood will be on their own head."-Leviticus 20:9. Notice that in this verse, we have both Descriptive and Prescriptive passages. We are to prescriptively obey our parents but descriptively know that God has issued a commandment to the people of Israel concerning the parent and child relationship. We know that disobedient children should not be killed because God gave us common sense through the law of logical inference. In addition, we do not have passages addressed to New Testament Christians commanding us to put our disobedient children on death row.

The same principle of obeying parents is found in the New Testament.

Children, obey your parents in the Lord, for this is right. "Honor your father and mother"—which is the first commandment with a promise—"so that it may go well with you and that you may enjoy long life on the earth."-Ephesians 6:1-3

Learning the difference between Descriptive and Prescriptive text will allow us to properly interpret Biblical passages.

Amen!

Bible Study Guideline

A. OBSERVATION- What does the scripture or passage say?

To help with observation, try asking the following questions:

Who are the characters involved?
- The writer
- The recipients
- The characters involved in the action

What are the key truths or events of the passage?
- Key ideas
- Important words

When did these things take place?
- Date of authorship
- Duration of the action
- When in biblical history
- Past, present, or future?

Where did these things take place?
- Places mentioned
- Buildings
- Cities
- Nations
- Landmarks

B. INTERPRETATION- What does it mean?

In order to help with interpretation, stick to the five C's of interpretation:

Content. The more time you spend in observation the more familiar you should be with the content of the passage! The content is all of the words, places, people, ideas, expressions, etc. contained in the passage.

Context. What can the surrounding context of the passage add to your understanding of it?

Comparison. The Bible itself sheds light on its own meaning. Use cross-references in your Bible to seek further answers to your questions.

Consult. What do other study tools (commentaries, Bible dictionaries, Bible encyclopedias, etc.) say about the passage? This should only be done <u>AFTER</u> you've done your own observation and interpretation!

Conclusions. What final conclusions do you have about the passage? In other words, what do you think the CORRECT interpretation is?

C. APPLICATION- What does it mean to me? What was the intent of the author?

In order to help with the application, consider the three different ways a passage can be applied:

New Ways to think and believe. *What is the main thing the Lord would want me to know from this passage?*

New Things to do. *What is the main thing the Lord would have me do as a result of studying this passage?*

Confirmation that the way I'm thinking and believing and/or the thing(s) I'm doing are correct.

Literary Genres (Forms)

By the term "genre" we mean literary type. Understanding the genre of a particular body of work will aid the reader in better understanding the overall scope and message of the author. In other words, understanding the "genre" will help you to understand the rules of the game.

Is the text intended to be "allegorical" or "literal?"

Types of Genres

The following are types of genres found in the Bible. All of the following genres can be found in the Old Testament.

1. Apocalyptic
2. Epistolary
3. Historical

4. Poetic
5. Romantic
6. Wisdom

Hermeneutics

"The science and art of Biblical interpretation."

When one is trying to read the Bible for all is worth, one must consider the textual constructs. You should ask yourself, "How is the book or passage put together?" Answering this question will help you get on the right track regarding understanding.

Consider the following:

1. Theme
2. Plot
3. Poetry
4. Motifs-an idea that persists through the literature.
5. Meter-Rhythm organized into patterns.
6. Rhyme-The repetition of similar sounds.
7. Parallelism-using parts of a sentence that is similar in grammar, sentence structure, meter, sound, and meaning.

II. THE STRUCTURE OF THE BIBLE

In order to properly understand a portion of Scripture, one must understand its structure. The structure of the passage often reveals the grouping and emphasis of the author. Since we are looking at the Scriptures from a foreign, often Western perspective, it is vitally important to know the original intent. Why learn the language and customs of the Old and New Testament? The answer is simple. A credible linguist will tell you that something gets lost in translation when you go from one language to another. No language in the world transfers to the receptor language completely. In other words, there are words used in Hebrew as well as Greek that have no equivalency in English. As a result, we must often research the original language to learn the usage of the word and find the closest word in English for it (the passage) to make sense to us.

Introduction to the Old Testament

According to recent statistics, the Bible is the most purchased book in America. According to research conducted by Barna Research Group, nearly nine out of ten Americans own a Bible. However, it should be noted that just because someone owns a Bible does not necessarily mean they read it. The Bible is a valuable reading commodity that is often ignored.

Some are hesitant about reading the Bible because they are not certain how to approach it. Terms like Old Testament, New Testament, chapters, verses, prophecies, doctrine, atonement, sacrifice, holiness, and a sundry of Biblical verbiage are often intimidating for many Christians.

This reading material aims to help the reader better understand the Bible and how to use it for edification.

WHAT IS THE BIBLE?

The word bible comes from the Greek word **biblos** which means book. It is the inerrant (without error) word of God. It is God's word to humanity. The Bible contains God's message of salvation for all mankind. It is at times also referred to as the God's word or Scriptures.

It is divided into two testaments (Old and New Testaments). The Old Testament consists of 39 books, and the New Testament consists of 27. The total number of books is 66.

The Old Testament books

Groupings

The Hebrew Bible was usually divided into three categories. The writings were classified under the main heading of the Law, the Prophets, and the Writings. The Hebrew Old Testament is also, at times, called the Masoretic text due to the transmission by the Masorite scholars or Tanakh. The name Tanakh is derived from the use of the consonants from the three major divisions (Torah, Nevi'im, and Kethuvim). The "a" vowel is added, thus the name Tanakh.

THE HEBREW OLD TESTAMENT ARRANGEMENT/Structure **Please note that in ancient times, the Hebrew bible was at times grouped differently.		
The Law (**T**orah)	The Prophets (**N**evi'im)	The Writings (**K**ethuvim)

1. Genesis
2. Exodus
3. Leviticus
4. Numbers
5. Deuteronomy
	A. Former Prophets
	  1. Joshua
	  2. Judges
	  3. Samuel
	    (1st & 2nd)
	  4. Kings (1st & 2nd)
	
	B. Latter Prophets
	  1. Isaiah
	  2. Jeremiah
	  3. Ezekiel
	  4. The Twelve
	    (one unit)
	    a. Hosea
	    b. Joel
	    c. Amos
	    d. Obadiah
	    e. Jonah
	    f. Micah
	    g. Nahum
	    h. Habbakuk
	    i. Zephaniah
	    j. Haggai
	    k. Zecharia
	    l. Malachi
		A. Poetical Books
		  1. Psalms
		  2. Proverbs
		  3. Job
		B. Five Rolls
		  (Megilloth)
		  1. Ruth
		  2. Song of Songs
		  3. Ecclesiastes
		  4. Lamentations
		  5. Esther
		C. Historical Books:
		  1. Daniel
		  2. Ezra-Nehemi-
		    ah (one unit)
		  3. Chronicles

During the time of Moses the Old Testament was called the covenant (Exodus 24:8). It was later referred to as the new covenant by Jeremiah (Jeremiah 31:31-34).

Transmission

The Old Testament (the Jewish Bible) is the New Testament concealed. In other words, the Old Testament (OT) is foundational for the Christian. We cannot fully understand the teachings of the New Testament without the Old Testament. As a result, Bible students must apply themselves in properly studying the Old Testament. Since the Old Testament is written in Hebrew and Aramaic, Bible students must learn how to handle the native language. This is the reason why is imperative for those who do not speak Hebrew and Aramaic to use Bible tools. Bible tools such as Bible dictionaries and lexicons were created to help us discover the original and intended meaning of the Scriptures.

The Old Testament was passed down to us prior to writing through oral means. In other words, the stories were originally passed down from person to person through speech. Since the Old Testament was originally written in Hebrew and Aramaic, you may be asking, "How did we get it in its present form?" It was first translated from Hebrew to Greek during the 3rd to 2nd Century BC. This translation from Hebrew to Greek is called the Septuagint. It is also at times referred to by the Latin letters (LXX), which represent 70. It is believed by some that 70 scholars (Masoretes) were responsible for translating the Old Testament Bible into Greek during the Middle Ages. It is due to the groupings of the Septuagint that we derived the total of Old Testament books. In addition, the books were positioned by subject matter.

For Example:

The following is the order of the Tanakh (The Jewish Bible) in contrast to the Christian Bible.

HEBREW OLD TESTAMENT	CHRISTIAN OLD TESTAMENT
The Books of Moses [Chumash]-(5 Books)	**The Law (5 Books)**
Genesis	Genesis
Exodus	Exodus
Leviticus	Leviticus
Numbers	Numbers
Deuteronomy	Deuteronomy
The Books of Prophets [Nevi'im]-(8 Books)	**History (12 Books)**
Joshua	Joshua
Judges	Judges
Samuel (1st & 2nd)	Ruth
Kings (1st & 2nd)	1 Samuel
Isaiah	2 Samuel
Jeremiah	1 Kings
Ezekiel	2 Kings
The twelve minor prophets (Trei-Assar): • Hosea, Joel, Amos, Obadiah, Jonah, Micah, Nahum, Habbakuk, Zephaniah, Haggai, Zechariah, Malachi	1 Chronicles
The Books of Writings (11 Books)	2 Chronicles
Psalms (Tehilim)	Ezra
Proverbs (Mishlei)	Nehemiah
Job (Iyov)	Esther
Song of Songs (Shir HaShirim)	**Poetry (5 Books)**
Ruth (Rus)	Job
Lamentations (Eicha)	Psalms

Ecclesiastes (Koheles)	Proverbs
Esther	Ecclesiastes
Daniel (Doniel)	Song of Solomon
Ezra/Nehemiah	**Prophets (17 Books)**
Chronicles	**A. Major**
	1. Isaiah 2. Jeremiah 3. Lamentations 4. Ezekiel 5. Daniel
	B. Minor
	1. Hosea 2. Joel 3. Amos 4. Obadiah 5. Jonah 6. Micah 7. Nahum 8. Habakkuk 9. Zephaniah 10. Haggai 11. Zechariah 12. Malachi

Old Testament Themes

For an introduction to the Old Testament, read "Survey of the Old Testament" by Paul N. Benware (1993)

The chart is an adaption of previous work by Professor Thomas Howe of Southern Evangelical Seminary

BOOK	THEME
Genesis	"The Book of Beginnings (universe, creation of man, sin, & redemption)"
Exodus	"The Redemption and Sanctification of God's People"

Leviticus	"The Sanctification of God's People"
Numbers	"The Testing of God's People"
Deuteronomy	"The Preparation and Instruction of God's People"
Joshua	"No Matter How Hard it May Seem, God Keeps His Promises"
Judges	"Despite Israel's Unfaithfulness, God is Faithful"
Ruth	"God Will Keep His Promises and Keep a Remnant to Fulfill His Promises"
1 Samuel 2 Samuel 1 Kings 2 Kings	"The Rise and Fall of Israel's Monarchy"
1 Chronicles 2 Chronicles	"The Sovereignty OF God in Preserving His People and Bringing them into the Land"
Ezra Nehemiah	"The Faithfulness of God to Keep His Covenant Promise and to Keep His Prophetic Word that He Would Restore Israel's Fortunes"
Esther	"The Providential Care of God in Preserving His People"
Job	"Why Do the Righteous Suffer?"

Psalms	"The Book of Praises"
Proverbs	"The Book of Wisdom Based on Godly Principles"
Ecclesiastes	"Life is Meaningless (Vain) Unless One Lives for God"
Song of Solomon	"The Sanctity and Rhapsody of Sexual Love as Shared in the Marriage Relationship"
Isaiah	"Yahweh is Our Salvation"
Jeremiah	"The Throwing Down of the People of God in Judgment for their Sins and the Re-establishment of the People of God in the Future Blessings of the Messianic Kingdom"
Lamentations	"Hope in God"
Ezekiel	"God Strengthens"
Daniel	"God is My Judge"
Hosea	"The Salvation (Deliverance) of Israel"
Joel	"Yahweh is God"
Amos	"The Judgment of Israel"

Obadiah	"God Will Bless those that Bless Israel and Curse those who Curse Israel"
Jonah	"The Grace of God is for those who Believe in God"
Micah	"Who is Yahweh?"
Nahum	"God Will Bring Consolation to His People"
Habbakuk	"The Righteous Must Live According to Faith by Trusting in God and Doing What is Righteous"
Zephaniah	"The Day of Yahweh"
Haggai	"The Return to the Lord as the Focus of Israel's Lives"
Zechariah	"God Remembers His People"
Malachi	"The Coming of the Angel of the Lord who is the Messenger of the Covenant and will Lead God's People into the Kingdom"

Example of Parallelism:

A. Synonymous Parallelism

b	a
He does not deal with us	According to our sins,
a'	b'
Nor repay us	According to our iniquities
	Psalms 103:10

B. Antithetical Parallelism (the second line restates the first as a contrast)

a	b	c	d	e
A	Wise	child	Gladdens	a Father
-a	-b	-c	-d	-e
(but) A	Foolish	Son	Grieves	His/her Mother
				Proverbs 10:1

NOTES: _____

_____

_____

_____

Example of Chiastic Structure of Noah chapters 6-9 (by Professor Howe of SES)

A . Noah (6:10A)
B ..... Schem, Ham, and Japheth (6:10b)
C .... Ark to be built (6:14-16)
D .... Flood Announced (6:17)
E .... Covenant with Noah (6:18-20)
F .... Food in the Ark (6:21)
G .... Command to Enter the Ark (7:1-3)
H .... 7 days waiting for Flood (7:4-5)
I .... 7 days waiting for Flood (7:7-10)
J .... Entry into Ark (7:11-15)
K .... Yahweh shuts door of Ark (7:16)
L .... 40 days of Flood (7:17a)
M .... Waters increase (7:17b-18)
N .... Mountains covered (7:19-20)
O .... 150 days waters prevail (7:21-24)
P .... God REMEMBERED NOAH (8:1)
O' .... 150 days water abate (8:3)
N' .... Mountains visible (8:4-5)
M' .... Waters abate (8:5)
L' .... 40 days, end of Rain (8:6a)
K' .... Noah opens window of Ark (8:6b)
J' .... Raven and dove leave Ark (8:7-9)
I' .... 7 days waiting for water to subside (8:10-11)

H'	7 days waiting for water to subside (8:12-13)
G'	Command to leave the Ark (8:15-17)
F'	Food outside the Ark (9:1-4)
E'	Covenant with all flesh (9:8-10)
D'	No Flood in future (9:11-17)
C'	Ark to be left (9:18a)
B'	Shem, Ham and Japheth (9:18b)
A'	Noah (9:19)

¹⁷ Think not that I am come to destroy the law, or the prophets: I am not come to destroy, but to fulfil.

¹⁸ For verily I say unto you, Till heaven and earth pass, one jot or one tittle shall in no wise pass from the law, till all be fulfilled.

¹⁹ Whosoever therefore shall break one of these least commandments, and shall teach men so, he shall be called the least in the kingdom of heaven: but whosoever shall do and teach them, the same shall be called great in the kingdom of heaven.

²⁰ For I say unto you, That except your righteousness shall exceed the righteousness of the scribes and Pharisees, ye shall in no case enter into the kingdom of heaven.–Matthew 5:17-20

The New Testament is peppered with many allusions to Old Testament passages. It is beneficial to first know the Old Testament referent in order to properly understand some New Testament scriptures.

For Example:

1. The prophet Elijah is mentioned at least 30 times in the New Testament (KJV). In order to properly interpret the passages, we must first learn about the Elijah narrative.
(Matt.11:14;16:14;17:3;17:4;17:10;17:11;17:12;

THE NEW TESTAMENT

The Structure of the New Testament

The New Testament contains 27 books of the Bible. It contains the gospels regarding the life of Jesus and the epistles mostly written by the apostle Paul. The New Testament is mostly written in Classical Greek and Aramaic. Some of the authors used scribes called amanuensis (e.g., Romans 16:22). Paul, despite using an amanuensis at times, chose to write the letters himself (e.g., Philemon 1:19). The apostle Mark, according to early church Father Papias, served as the scribe for the apostle Peter.

The gospels of Matthew, Mark, and Luke are called synoptic. The word synoptic means similar, and many of the stories documented in these three books are similar. However, the gospel of John stands alone due to its uniqueness.

NOTES:

The structure of the New Testament is as follows:

Book	Author	Date	Location of Writing	Theme
Matthew	Matthew	AD 66-68	Antioch of Syria	Jesus, the Messianic King.
Mark	Mark	AD 64-65	Rome	Christ, the Suffering Servant.
Luke	Luke	AD 57-60	Outside of Palestine	Jesus, the Son of Man.
John	John	AD 90-95	Ephesus	Jesus, the Messiah & Son of God.
Acts	Luke	AD 66-67	Outside of Palestine	Jesus, the Risen Glorified Lord Over His Church.
Romans	Paul	AD 57	Corinth	The Righteousness of God.
1 Corinthians	Paul	AD 54	Ephesus	The Wisdom of God as Seen in the Message of the Cross & the Resurrection of Christ Applied to the Total Life of the Church.
2nd Corinthians	Paul	AD 55-56	Ephesus	The Defense of Paul's Apostolic Credentials, Authority and Message.
Galatians	Paul	AD 48	Syrian/Antioch	Christian Liberty in Christ through the Gospel of Grace.

Ephesians	Paul	AD 60-61	Rome	The Church, the body of Christ
Philippians	Paul		Rome	Joyful Unity in Christ as a Faithful Testimony of the Gospel.
Colossians	Paul	AD 60-61	Rome	The Pre-Eminence and Sufficiency of Christ, the Head of the Church.
1 Thessalonians	Paul	AD 50	Corinth	The Return of Christ, the Hope of the Believer.
2 Thessalonians	Paul	AD 50	Corinth	The Day of the Lord, the Believer's Ultimate Vindication.
1 Timothy	Paul	AD 62	Macedonia	Conduct in the Household of God, the Church of the Living God, the Pillar and Support of the Truth.
2 Timothy	Paul	AD 64	Rome	The Character and Conduct of the Servant Minister of Christ.
Titus	Paul	AD 62	Ephesus	The Church and the Ministry.
Philemon	Paul	AD 60-61	Roman	Fellowship and Forgiveness in Christ.

Are There Bible Contradictions: An Apologetic Response

Hebrews	Anonymous**	AD 64	Unknown	The High Priestly Ministry of God's Royal Messianic Son.
James	James	AD 61-62	Jerusalem	The Testing/Trials of the Believer's Faith.
1 Peter	Peter	AD 65	Rome	Suffering in Grace.
2 Peter	Peter	AD 65-67	Rome	Growing in Grace.
1 John	John	AD 85-100	Ephesus	Fellowship with God the Father and with His Son Jesus Christ.
2 John	John	AD 85-100	Ephesus	Walking in Apostolic Doctrine.
3 John	John	AD 85-100	Ephesus	Walking in Apostolic Truth.
Jude	Jude	AD 67-68	Unknown	Contending for the Faith Once For All Delivered.
Revelation	John	AD 81-96	Patmos, Greece	Jesus Christ Coming Worldwide Judgement and Kingdom Reign.

New Testament Themes

The following chart was adapted from Dr. Thomas Howe of SES lecture Notes.

BOOK	THEME
Matthew	"Jesus, the Messianic King"
Mark	"Christ, the Suffering Servant"
Luke	"Jesus, the Son of Man"

John	"Jesus, the Messiah and Son of God"
Acts	"Jesus, the Risen Glorified Lord Over His Church"
Romans	"The Righteousness of God"
1 Corinthians	"The Wisdom of God, As Seen in the Message of the Cross and the Resurrection of Christ, Applied to the Total Life of the Church"
2 Corinthians	"The Defense of Paul's Apostolic Credentials, Authority and Message"
Galatians	"Christian Liberty in Christ through the Gospel of Grace"
Ephesians	"The Church, the Body of Christ"
Philippians	"Joyful Unity in Christ as a Faithful Testimony of the Gospel"
Colossians	"The Preeminence and Sufficiency of Christ, the Head of the Church"
1 Thessalonians	"The Return of Christ, the Hope of the Believer"
2 Thessalonians	"The Day of the Lord, the Believer's Ultimate Vindication"
1 Timothy	"Conduct in the Household of God, the Church of the Living God, the Pillar and Support of the Truth"
2 Timothy	"The Character and Conduct of the Servant-Minister of Christ"

Titus	"The Church and the Ministry"
Philemon	"Fellowship and Forgiveness in Christ"
Hebrews	"The High Priestly Ministry of God's Royal Messianic Son"
James	"The Testing/Trials of the Believer's Faith"
1 Peter	"Suffering in Grace"
2 Peter	"Growing in Grace"
1 John	"Fellowship with God the Father and with His Son Jesus Christ"
2 John	"Walking in Apostolic Doctrine"
3 John	"Walking in Apostolic Truth"
Jude	"Contending for the Faith "Once For All Delivered"
Revelation	"Jesus Christ's Coming Worldwide Judgment and Kingdom Reign"

There are two questions concerning the New Testament:

1. Do we have what they wrote?
2. Are what they wrote accurate?

The answer to both questions is a resounding YES! We do have what the apostles wrote and yes, the writings that we have are accurate. In order to find out the trustworthiness of ancient manuscripts, it is helpful to find other copies. In other words, when scholars have more copies of a particular text they are better able to discern what the passage is saying and also able to determine its authenticity. The New Testament manuscripts rank high among other ancient manuscripts. There are more New Testament manuscripts than any other ancient documents. Observe the table below:

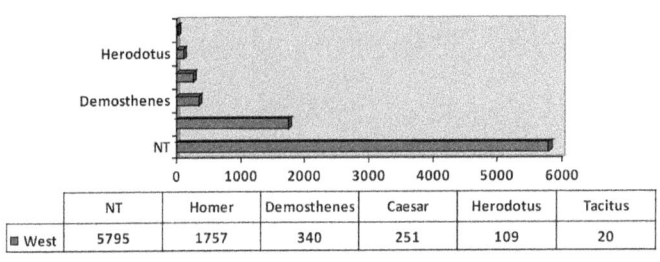

	NT	Homer	Demosthenes	Caesar	Herodotus	Tacitus
West	5795	1757	340	251	109	20

Homer (ca. 8th Century BC)	Composed the Iliad and the Odyssey.
Demosthenes (4th Century BC)	Orator who wrote about the Greek life.
Tacitus (2nd Century AD)	Roman historian and author.
Cæsar (1st Century BC)	Roman Dictator, General, and author of war stories.
Herodotus (5th Century BC)	The father of History and wrote systematized historical data.

III. Bible Study Tools

The Bible is clear about reading and studying God's word (1 Peter 3:15). Christians should always read the Bible for enjoyment and exposure. However, it is also necessary to study the Bible. Studying the Bible requires the believer to dig deeper into the Scriptures as it relates to culture, language, economics, and other subjects.

How do we learn about what happened 2000-plus years ago? You can go to local Bible studies, seminary, or a Bible college in order to learn more about the Bible. The fact is some subjects can take a lifetime to research and investigate. However, in many cases, we do not need to reinvent the wheel. God has allowed other believers to lay the groundwork as it relates to research in specific areas. The compilation of these works is often called Bible tools.

The following information is certainly not an exhaustive list, but it will help you in studying the word of God.

SPECIFIC BIBLE STUDY TOOLS

	Strong's Concordance of the Bible: This concordance contains the Hebrew and Greek lexicon in connection with the King James Version of the Bible. This concordance can be a valuable tool if you are attempting to look up a Scripture or dig up the original meaning of the word.
	Nelson's Illustrated Bible Companion: This picture encyclopedia contains not only pictures but historical data, archaeological data, and background of the various stories found in the Bible. Moreover, readers will get a summary of the books of the Bible. The pictures of the Bible lands are incredible!

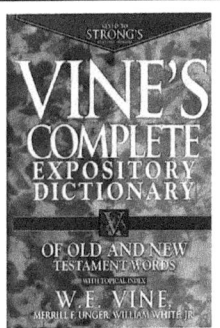	Vine's Expository Dictionary of the Bible: Vine's expository dictionary is a great tool for Bible study. Users can find the English equivalent meaning of the New Testament Greek word. It can also be used in conjunction with the Strong's concordance.
	Logos Bible software is an online Bible study tool. It can be accessed by using your phone, tablet, or home desktop. Logos was designed for Christians who are interested in true Biblical scholarship. The word study and etymology mode is only two of the many features you will find. Many Biblical scholars use Logos for their research. It is a bit expensive but worth every penny.
	The Holman Bible Atlas: The Holman Bible Atlas contains 140 photographs of Bible lands. The pictures allow modern Christians to see the Bible lands without having to visit those locations.

	The Interlinear Bible: This book contains Strong's Hebrew & Greek Lexicon. It provides a literal translation of the original language of the Bible with the English translation underneath the passages. It contains analytical lexicons as well as concordances. For those desiring to view the original language in its true form this book is highly recommended.

GLOSSARY

Eschatology-The study of the last days or future events.

Exegesis-The process for interpreting a text. This method teaches the reader to pull out of the text what is already there.

Genre-A type or style of literature.

Hermeneutics-The Science and art of Biblical interpretation. These are the rules one must use to properly interpret Scripture.

Inerrant-The Bible is free from error. The idea that the Bible does not affirm anything that is contradictory.

Paradox-Assumed or perceived contradictions of Scripture.

Parallelism-A term often used in Hebrew poetry which signifies the relationship between successive poetic lines.

Transmission-The copying of a text.

ABOUT THE AUTHOR

Perseus Poku served for 18 years as the staff minister at St. Paul Baptist Church (Sacramento, CA). During his tenure as Staff Minister, he also led the Bible Answer Ministry for 10 years. He has an A.A. in Education from Cosumnes River College, a B.A. in History from California State University, and a Masters in Christian apologetics from Southern Evangelical Seminary.

Are There Bible Contradictions: An Apologetic Response

He is the founder of **Sound Reasoning Ministries** which provides training on how to articulate and defend the basic tenets of Christianity. In addition, Mr. Poku has over thirty-two years of training Christians on sound doctrine. He is the author of the book entitled "Bible Answers to 110 Doctrinal Questions." He has written articles for the Christian Research Journal as well as Logos Bible Word for Word platform. Furthermore, he is the host of the weekly radio show *"SOUND REASONING."*

Perseus is highly recommended by Christian authors and theologians such as the late Dr. Norman Geisler, J.P. Moreland, and Sean Mcdowell.

www.ingramcontent.com/pod-product-compliance
Lightning Source LLC
Chambersburg PA
CBHW060430050426
42449CB00009B/2226